Get your facts straight with CGP!

This CGP Knowledge Organiser has one mission in life —
helping you remember the key facts for AQA GCSE Physics.

We've boiled every topic down to the vital definitions,
facts and diagrams, making it all easy to memorise.

There's also a matching Knowledge Retriever book that'll test
you on every page. Perfect for making sure you know it all!

CGP — still the best! ☺

Our sole aim here at CGP is to produce the highest quality books —
carefully written, immaculately presented and dangerously close to being funny.

Then we work our socks off to get them out to you
— at the cheapest possible prices.

Contents

This book only contains the equations that you need to remember.
All other equations will be given to you in the exam.

Published by CGP.
From original material by Richard Parsons.

Editors: Georgina Fairclough, Emily Garrett, Luke Molloy and Sarah Williams.
Contributors: Ian Francis and Paddy Gannon.

With thanks to Mark Edwards and Duncan Lindsay for the proofreading.
With thanks to Emily Smith for the copyright research.

ISBN: 978 1 78908 490 0

Data used to construct stopping distance graph on page 36 from the Highway Code.
Contains public sector information licensed under the Open Government Licence v3.0.
http://www.nationalarchives.gov.uk/doc/open-government-licence/version/3/

Printed by Elanders Ltd, Newcastle upon Tyne.
Clipart from Corel®
Illustrations by: Sandy Gardner Artist, email sandy@sandygardner.co.uk

Text, design, layout and original illustrations © Coordination Group Publications Ltd (CGP) 2020
All rights reserved.

The Scientific Method

Developing Theories

Come up with hypothesis

↓

Test hypothesis

↓

Evidence is peer-reviewed

↓

If all evidence backs up hypothesis, it becomes an accepted theory.

HYPOTHESIS — a possible explanation for an observation.

PEER REVIEW — when other scientists check results and explanations before they're published.

Accepted theories can still change over time as more evidence is found, e.g. the theory of atomic structure:

Models

REPRESENTATIONAL MODELS — a simplified description or picture of the real system, e.g. the molecular model of matter:

solid liquid gas

Models help scientists explain observations and make predictions.

COMPUTATIONAL MODELS — computers are used to simulate complex processes.

Issues in Science

Scientific developments can create four issues:

1 Economic — e.g. beneficial technology, like alternative energy sources, may be too expensive to use.

2 Environmental — e.g. new technology could harm the natural environment.

3 Social — decisions based on research can affect society, e.g. taxes on fossil fuels.

4 Personal — some decisions affect individuals, e.g. a person may not want a wind farm being built near to their home.

Media reports on scientific developments may be oversimplified, inaccurate or biased.

Hazard and Risk

HAZARD — something that could potentially cause harm.

RISK — the chance that a hazard will cause harm.

Hazards associated with physics experiments include:

 Eye damage from lasers.

Faulty electrical equipment.

Fire from Bunsen burners.

The seriousness of the harm and the likelihood of it happening both need consideration.

Designing & Performing Experiments

Collecting Data

Data should be...		
REPEATABLE	Same person gets same results after repeating experiment using the same method and equipment.	
REPRODUCIBLE	Similar results can be achieved by someone else, or by using a different method or piece of equipment.	
ACCURATE	Results are close to the true answer.	
PRECISE	All data is close to the mean.	

Reliable data is repeatable and reproducible.

Valid results are repeatable and reproducible and answer the original question.

Fair Tests

INDEPENDENT VARIABLE	Variable that you change.
DEPENDENT VARIABLE	Variable that is measured.
CONTROL VARIABLE	Variable that is kept the same.
CONTROL EXPERIMENT	An experiment kept under the same conditions as the rest of the investigation without anything being done to it.
FAIR TEST	An experiment where only the independent variable changes, whilst all other variables are kept the same.

Controller variables

Control experiments are carried out when variables can't be controlled.

Four Things to Look Out For

1. RANDOM ERRORS — unpredictable differences caused by things like human errors in measuring.
2. SYSTEMATIC ERRORS — measurements that are wrong by the same amount each time.
3. ZERO ERRORS — systematic errors that are caused by using a piece of equipment that isn't zeroed properly.
4. ANOMALOUS RESULTS — results that don't fit with the rest of the data.

Anomalous results can be ignored if you know what caused them.

Processing Data

Calculate the mean — add together all data values and divide by number of values.

UNCERTAINTY — the amount by which a given result may differ from the true value.

$$\text{uncertainty} = \frac{\text{range}}{2}$$

largest value minus smallest value

In any calculation, you should round the answer to the lowest number of significant figures (s.f.) given.

Working Scientifically

Presenting Data

Bar Charts

Bar charts are used when independent variable is categoric or discrete.

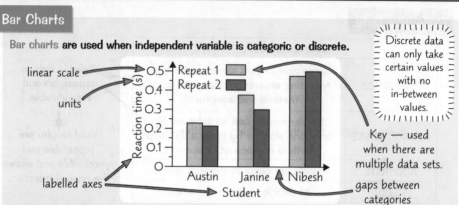

Discrete data can only take certain values with no in-between values.

linear scale

units

labelled axes

Key — used when there are multiple data sets.

gaps between categories

Plotting Graphs

Graphs are used when both variables are continuous.

Continuous data — can take any numerical value within a range.

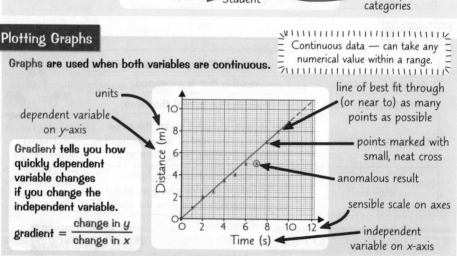

units

dependent variable on y-axis

Gradient tells you how quickly dependent variable changes if you change the independent variable.

$$\text{gradient} = \frac{\text{change in } y}{\text{change in } x}$$

line of best fit through (or near to) as many points as possible

points marked with small, neat cross

anomalous result

sensible scale on axes

independent variable on x-axis

Three Types of Correlation Between Variables

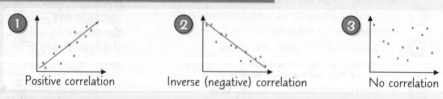

Positive correlation

Inverse (negative) correlation

No correlation

Possible reasons for a correlation:

Chance — correlation might be a fluke.

Third variable — another factor links the two variables.

Cause — if every other variable that could affect the result is controlled, you can conclude that changing one variable causes the change in the other.

Working Scientifically

Conclusions, Evaluations and Units

Conclusions

Draw conclusion by stating relationship between dependent and independent variables.

↓

Justify conclusion using specific data.

↓

Refer to original hypothesis and state whether data supports it.

You can only draw a conclusion from what your data shows — you can't go any further than that.

Evaluations

EVALUATION — a critical analysis of the whole investigation.

	Things to consider
Method	• Validity of method • Control of variables
Results	• Reliability, accuracy, precision and reproducibility of results • Number of measurements taken • Level of uncertainty in the results
Anomalous results	• Causes of any anomalous results

You could make more predictions based on your conclusion, which you could test in future experiments.

Repeating experiment with changes to improve the quality of results will give you more confidence in your conclusions.

S.I. Units

S.I. BASE UNITS — a set of standard units that all scientists use.

Quantity		S.I. Unit
🔩	mass	kilogram (kg)
📏	length	metre (m)
⏱	time	second (s)
🌡	temperature	kelvin (K)

Scaling Units

SCALING PREFIX — a word or symbol that goes before a unit to indicate a multiplying factor.

Multiple of unit	Prefix
10^{12}	tera (T)
10^{9}	giga (G)
10^{6}	mega (M)
1000	kilo (k)
0.1	deci (d)
0.01	centi (c)
0.001	milli (m)
10^{-6}	micro (μ)
10^{-9}	nano (n)

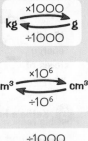

kg $\xrightarrow{\times 1000}$ g, $\div 1000$

m³ $\xrightarrow{\times 10^{6}}$ cm³, $\div 10^{6}$

kg/m³ $\xrightarrow{\div 1000}$ g/cm³, $\times 1000$

Working Scientifically

Energy Stores, Transfers and Systems

Eight Types of Energy Store

1. Kinetic
2. Gravitational potential
3. Elastic potential
4. Electrostatic
5. Thermal (internal)
6. Chemical
7. Magnetic
8. Nuclear

Four Types of Energy Transfer

1. Mechanical (a force doing work)
2. Electrical (work done by moving charges)
3. Heating
4. Radiation (e.g. light or sound)

Work done = energy transferred.

Energy Transfers in Five Different Systems

SYSTEM — a single object or a group of objects.

1 Arm throwing ball up

Chemical energy store of arm.

↓ force exerted by arm does work

Kinetic energy store of ball and arm.

2 Ball falling

Gravitational potential energy store of ball.

↓ gravitational force does work

Kinetic energy store of ball.

3 Brakes applied to car wheels

Kinetic energy stores of wheels. — friction does work → Thermal energy stores of surroundings.

4 Car hitting tree

Kinetic energy store of car.

↓ normal contact force does work

Other energy stores — e.g. elastic potential energy stores of car and tree.

5 Kettle's heating element and water

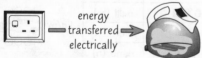

energy transferred electrically ⇒ Thermal energy store of kettle's heating element. — energy transferred by heating ⇒ Thermal energy store of water.

Energy, Power and Efficiency

Kinetic Energy

kinetic energy (J)

$$E_k = \frac{1}{2}mv^2$$

mass (kg)   speed (m/s)

Gravitational Potential Energy

mass (kg)

gravitational potential energy (J) $E_p = mgh$ height (m)

gravitational field strength (N/kg)

Conservation of Energy and Specific Heat Capacity

CONSERVATION OF ENERGY — energy can be transferred usefully, stored or dissipated but not created or destroyed.

Energy transferred usefully (by heating) to thermal energy store of pot, increasing its temperature.

Some energy dissipated as energy transferred to thermal energy stores of surroundings.

In all systems, energy is dissipated (wasted) to a store that's not useful (usually thermal).

 SPECIFIC HEAT CAPACITY — the amount of energy needed to raise the temperature of 1 kg of a substance by 1 °C.

CLOSED SYSTEM — no energy (or matter) is transferred in or out of the system, so there is no overall change in total energy.

Power

POWER — rate of energy transfer (or rate of doing work).
One watt (W) = one joule of energy transferred per second.

energy transferred (J)

$$P = \frac{E}{t}$$

power (W)   time (s)

work done (J)

$$P = \frac{W}{t}$$

power (W)   time (s)

2 W motor transfers more energy per second than 1 W motor, so lifts mass faster.

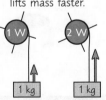

Efficiency Equations

Revision efficiency can be increased with tea and biscuits (probably).

$$\text{Efficiency} = \frac{\text{Useful output energy transfer}}{\text{Total input energy transfer}}$$

$$\text{Efficiency} = \frac{\text{Useful power output}}{\text{Total power input}}$$

No device is 100% efficient.

Multiply by 100 to get a percentage.

Topic 1 — Energy

8

Reducing Unwanted Energy Transfers

Conduction

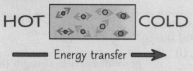

HOT COLD

━━━ Energy transfer ➡

CONDUCTION — process where vibrating particles transfer energy to neighbouring particles.

Convection

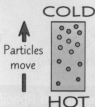

COLD

Particles move

HOT

CONVECTION — where energetic particles move from hotter to cooler regions.

Lubrication and Thermal Insulation

Frictional force acts between moving gears, so energy dissipated (an unwanted energy transfer).

Apply lubricant (e.g. oil).

Frictional force reduced so energy dissipated reduced.

Thermal insulation (e.g. cotton wool) reduces unwanted energy transfers by heating.

Lubrication and thermal insulation increase the efficiency of useful energy transfers.

Two Ways to Decrease How Quickly a Building Cools

1 Increase thickness of its walls.

2 Make walls out of material with lower thermal conductivity.

The higher a material's thermal conductivity, the faster it transfers energy by conduction.

Non-Renewables and Renewables

Non-Renewable and Renewable Energy Resources

NON-RENEWABLE ENERGY RESOURCES — energy resources that will run out one day.
RENEWABLE ENERGY RESOURCES — energy resources that will never run out.

 All energy resources used to generate electricity.

 Some energy resources used for heating and transport.

Three Fossil Fuels Non-renewable

1 Coal

Burned for heating and used to power steam trains.

2 Oil

Used to make fuel (petrol and diesel) for cars.

3 (Natural) Gas

Used to heat water that is then pumped into radiators.

Fossil fuels are burned to generate electricity.

- Burning fossil fuels releases CO_2, contributing to global warming.
- Burning coal and oil releases sulfur dioxide, causing acid rain.

R Reliable

Nuclear Power Non-renewable

Nuclear fuel undergoes fission in nuclear reactors, generating electricity.

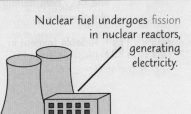

- Nuclear waste is dangerous and difficult to dispose of.
- Carries the risk of a major catastrophe.

R Reliable

Wind Power Renewable

Wind turns wind turbines, generating electricity.

- Produce no pollution when in use.
- Noisy.
- Spoil the view.

 Unreliable
Turbines stop turning when wind stops or is too strong.

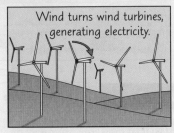

Renewables

Solar Power

 Renewable

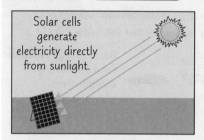

Solar cells generate electricity directly from sunlight.

- Produce no pollution when in use.

 Reliable (in daytime) especially in sunny countries.

Solar water heaters use the sun to heat water which is then pumped into radiators.

Geothermal Power

 Renewable

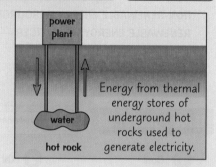

power plant

water

hot rock

Energy from thermal energy stores of underground hot rocks used to generate electricity.

- Do very little environmental damage.

 Reliable

Geothermal heat pumps are used to heat buildings.

Hydro-electric Power

 Renewable

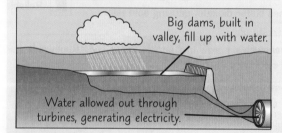

Big dams, built in valley, fill up with water.

Water allowed out through turbines, generating electricity.

- Produce no pollution when in use.
- Rotting plants (from flooding the valley) release methane and CO_2, contributing to global warming.

 Reliable (except in times of drought).

Wave Power

 Renewable

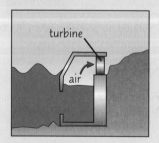

turbine

air

Waves move up and down. → Air forced through turbines. → Electricity generated.

- Produce no pollution when in use.
- Disturb habitats of sea animals.
- Spoil the view.

 Unreliable Waves depend on wind.

Renewables and Trends

Tidal Barrages Renewable

Tide comes in.

↓

Water builds behind the dam.

↓

Water allowed out through turbines. ⟶ Electricity generated.

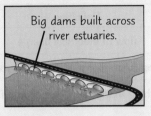
Big dams built across river estuaries.

- Produce no pollution when in use.
- Disturb habitats of nearby wildlife.
- Spoil the view.

R Reliable
Tides are predictable.

Bio-fuels Renewable

Made from plant products or animal dung.

Bio-fuels are burned to generate electricity.

- In some regions, large areas of forest destroyed to grow bio-fuels, so species lose natural habitats.

R Reliable

⎰⎰⎰ Bio-fuels are also burned for heating and used as fuel in some cars. ⎱⎱⎱

Trends in Energy Use

1900 – 2000 ⟹ Electricity use increased as:
- population grew and people began to use electricity for more things.

2000 onwards ⟹ Electricity use decreasing as:
- appliances are more efficient.
- people are more careful with amount of energy use.

Three reasons why we're increasing use of renewables:

1 Burning fossil fuels is very damaging to environment.

2 We need to learn how to get by without non-renewables before they run out.

3 Pressure on governments have led them to introduce renewable energy targets.

⎰⎰⎰ Scientists can advise others to use more renewables, but don't have the power to make things change. Change limited by cost, social issues, ethical concerns and political issues. ⎱⎱⎱

Current

Current, Potential Difference and Resistance

	Definition	Unit
CURRENT	flow of electrical charge	ampere, A
POTENTIAL DIFFERENCE	driving force that pushes charge round	volt, V
RESISTANCE	anything that slows down charge flow	ohm, Ω

Current in Circuits

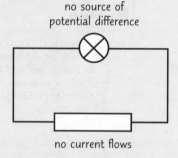

no source of
potential difference

no current flows

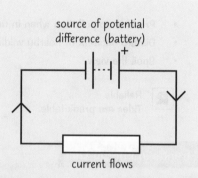

source of potential
difference (battery)

current flows

Current through a component depends on two factors:

 The component's resistance.

The greater the resistance, the smaller the current.

 The potential difference across the component.

The greater the potential difference, the larger the current (for a fixed resistance).

Charge in Circuits

size of the current = rate of flow of charge

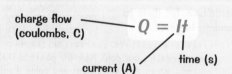

charge flow
(coulombs, C)

$$Q = It$$

current (A)   time (s)

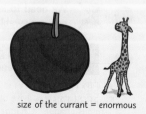

size of the currant = enormous

V = IR and Circuit Symbols

Potential Difference Equation

resistance (Ω)

potential difference (V) — $V = IR$

current (A)

Circuit Symbols

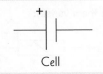

Cell

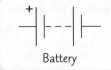

Battery

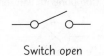

Switch open

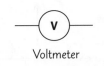

Voltmeter

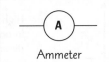

Ammeter

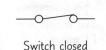

Switch closed

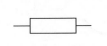

Resistor

Variable resistor

Filament lamp
(or bulb)

Diode

LDR (Light-
Dependent Resistor)

Thermistor

LED (Light-
Emitting Diode)

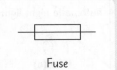

Fuse

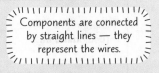

Components are connected
by straight lines — they
represent the wires.

I-V Characteristics and Circuit Devices

Three Different *I-V* Characteristics

1 Ohmic conductor (e.g. a resistor) ─▭─
at constant temperature

Current is directly proportional to potential difference...

... so resistance doesn't change.

This graph is linear.

Components with changing resistance (when current through them varies):

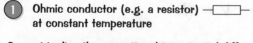

2 Filament lamp ─⊗─

Current increases...

... so temperature
of filament
increases...

... so resistance
increases.

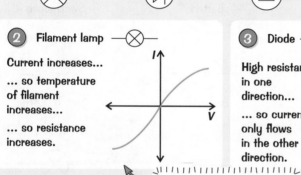

3 Diode ─▷|─

High resistance
in one
direction...

... so current
only flows
in the other
direction.

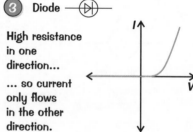

These graphs are non-linear.

LDRs and Thermistors

	LDR	Thermistor
Resistance depends on...	light intensity	temperature
Lower resistance in...	brighter light	hotter temperatures
Used in...	automatic night lights	thermostats

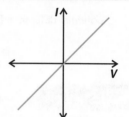

Series and Parallel Circuits

Series Circuits

Current is the same everywhere.
$$I_1 = I_2$$

Total source potential difference is shared between components.
$$V_{total} = V_1 + V_2$$

Total resistance of components = sum of their resistances.
$$R_{total} = R_1 + R_2$$

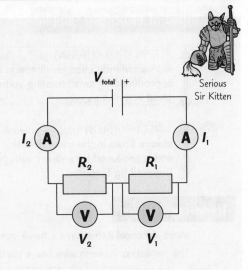

Serious Sir Kitten

Adding a resistor in series increases the total resistance of the circuit.

Parallel Circuits

Total current flowing around a circuit = sum of the currents through each branch.
$$I_{total} = I_1 + I_2$$

Potential difference across each branch is the same as the source potential difference.
$$V_1 = V_2 = V_{total}$$

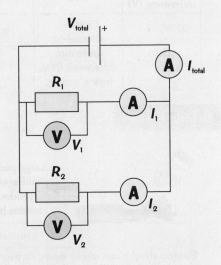

The total resistance of resistors in parallel is less than the resistance of the smallest resistor.

Adding a resistor in parallel decreases the total resistance of the circuit.

Electricity in the Home

Two Types of Electricity Supply

① **ALTERNATING CURRENT (ac)** — current that constantly changes direction and is produced by an alternating voltage. Used in mains supply.

② **DIRECT CURRENT (dc)** — current that always flows in the same direction and is produced by a direct voltage. Supplied by batteries.

Three Facts about UK Mains

① ac supply

② frequency of 50 Hz

③ voltage around 230 V

Three-core Cables

- Most electrical items have a three-core cable.
- The insulation on each wire has a particular colour to identify it.

earth
live
neutral

	live wire	neutral wire	earth wire
Colour	brown	blue	green and yellow
Potential difference (V)	230	around 0	0
Use	Provides alternating potential difference from mains supply.	Completes the circuit.	Stops appliance casing becoming live.

Current only flows through earth wire when there's a fault.

Electric Shocks

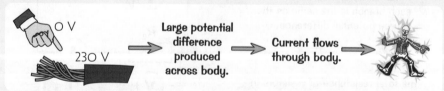

0 V

230 V

Large potential difference produced across body.

Current flows through body.

Electric shocks can cause injury or even death.

Even if a plug socket is turned off, there is still danger of an electric shock.

Any connection between the live wire and the earth can be dangerous — e.g. it could cause a fire.

Energy, Power and the National Grid

Energy Transfers

When charge flows, work is done (and so energy is transferred).

 Energy transferred electrically

to thermal energy store of the
heating element inside the kettle.

 Energy transferred electrically

to kinetic energy store of the fan's motor.

Energy

energy transferred (J)   charge flow (C)

$$E = QV$$ potential
difference (V)

Amount of energy an appliance
transfers depends on:

- appliance's power
- how long appliance is on for

energy transferred (J)   power (W)

$$E = Pt$$ time (s)

Power

POWER — energy transferred per second.

POWER RATING — maximum safe
power an appliance can operate at.

power (W)   potential
                 difference (V)

$$P = VI$$ current (A)

power (W)   current (A)

$$P = I^2R$$ resistance (Ω)

The National Grid

NATIONAL GRID — a system of cables and transformers
that connect power stations to consumers.

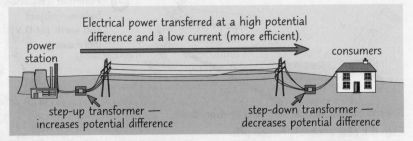

Electrical power transferred at a high potential
difference and a low current (more efficient).

power station   consumers

step-up transformer —
increases potential difference

step-down transformer —
decreases potential difference

Transferring at a high current would heat up the wires and transfer a lot of
energy to the thermal energy stores of the surroundings (not efficient).

Static Electricity

Static Charges

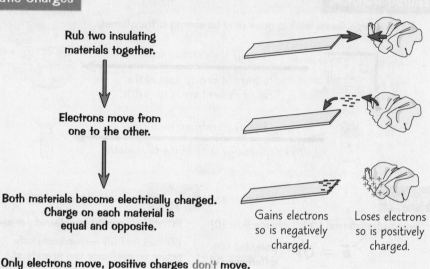

Rub two insulating materials together.

Electrons move from one to the other.

Both materials become electrically charged. Charge on each material is equal and opposite.

Gains electrons so is negatively charged.

Loses electrons so is positively charged.

Only electrons move, positive charges don't move.

Electric Sparks

ELECTRIC SPARK — the passage of electrons across a gap between a charged object and the earth (or an earthed conductor). (This usually happens when the gap is small.)

Three steps to an electric spark:

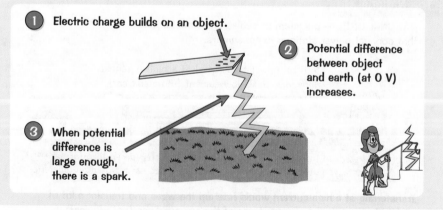

1 Electric charge builds on an object.

2 Potential difference between object and earth (at 0 V) increases.

3 When potential difference is large enough, there is a spark.

Electric Fields

Electric Fields Around Charged Spheres

ELECTRIC FIELD — a region in which another charged object feels a force.

An electric field is created around any electrically charged object.

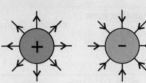

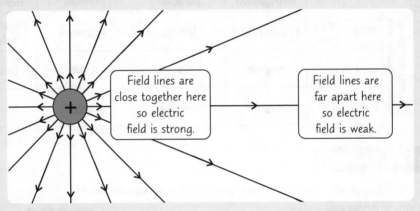

Field lines are close together here so electric field is strong.

Field lines are far apart here so electric field is weak.

Strong electric fields ionise air particles, which can cause sparks.

Attraction and Repulsion

When a charged object is placed in the electric field of another charged object, they both feel a force.

These are non-contact forces.

Attraction:

Repulsion:

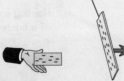

Bring charged object near suspended rod of same charge.

Suspended rod moves away from charged object.

As distance between charged objects decreases, force acting on the charges increases.

Density, States and Internal Energy

Density

DENSITY — mass per unit volume.

$$\rho = \frac{m}{V}$$

density (kg/m³)   mass (kg)   volume (m³)

States of Matter

		Particle arrangement	Forces between particles	Distance between particles	Particle motion
Density decreases	SOLID	Regular, fixed	Strong	Very small	Vibration only
	LIQUID	Irregular	Weak	Small	Slow
	GAS	Irregular	Very weak	Large	Fast

Changes of State

Changes of state are physical changes. Mass is always conserved.

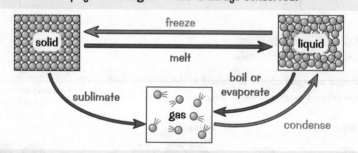

freeze

solid   liquid

melt

boil or evaporate

sublimate   condense

gas

Internal Energy

INTERNAL ENERGY — the total energy stored by the particles that make up a system.

Internal energy of a system = total amount of energy in kinetic and potential energy stores of all its particles

Heating

Heating increases the internal energy of a system.

This can do one of two things:

1 Increase the temperature

2 Change the state

Heating and Cooling

Heating Graphs

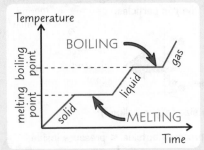

Temperature

BOILING

melting point | boiling point

solid

liquid

gas

MELTING

Time

Three things happen in melting and boiling:

1. Bonds between particles are broken.

2. Internal energy increases — energy is transferred to particles' potential energy stores.

3. Temperature stays the same.

Cooling Graphs

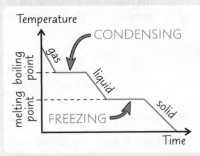

Temperature

CONDENSING

melting point | boiling point

gas

liquid

FREEZING

solid

Time

Three things happen in condensing and freezing:

1. Stronger bonds form between particles.

2. Internal energy decreases — energy is transferred away from particles' potential energy stores.

3. Temperature stays the same.

Specific Heat Capacity, Latent Heat and Specific Latent Heat

SPECIFIC HEAT CAPACITY — the amount of energy needed to raise the temperature of 1 kg of a substance by 1 °C.

LATENT HEAT — the energy needed to change the state of a substance.

SPECIFIC LATENT HEAT — the amount of energy needed to change 1 kg of a substance from one state to another, without changing its temperature.

 SPECIFIC LATENT HEAT OF FUSION — the specific latent heat of changing between a solid and a liquid.

 SPECIFIC LATENT HEAT OF VAPORISATION — the specific latent heat of changing between a liquid and a gas.

Topic 3 — Particle Model of Matter

Particle Motion in Gases

Gas Particles and Gas Pressure

 The higher the temperature of a gas, the higher the average energy in the kinetic energy stores of the gas particles.

Gas particles are constantly moving randomly.

Gas pressure is caused by gas particles colliding with a surface and exerting a net force on it.  Net force acts at right angles to the container wall.

For a gas inside a container that can change size (e.g. a balloon):

pressure outside > pressure inside

↓

gas is compressed

pressure outside < pressure inside

↓

gas expands

A Gas at Constant Volume

 Temperature increase

↓

Particles get faster and collide with the container more often.

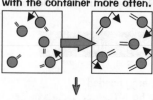

↓

Pressure increases

A Gas at Constant Temperature

 Volume increase

↓

Particles spread out and collide with the container less often.

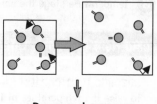

↓

Pressure decreases

Doing Work on Gases

Force is applied to gas. Work is done as energy is transferred. ⟹ Doing work on the gas increases its internal energy. ⟹ Temperature of an enclosed gas increases.

 Force is applied to air in bike pump and tyre.

 Internal energy of air in tyre increases.

 Tyre temperature increases.

Topic 3 — Particle Model of Matter

Developing the Model of the Atom

The History of the Atom

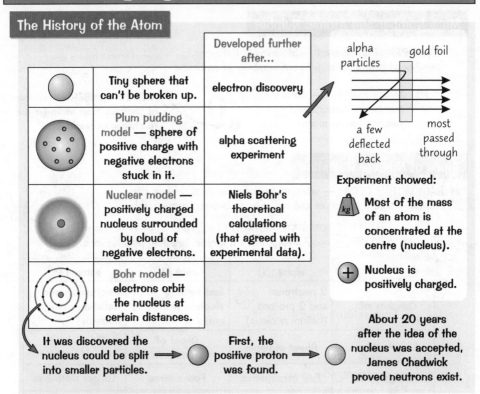

		Developed further after...
	Tiny sphere that can't be broken up.	electron discovery
	Plum pudding model — sphere of positive charge with negative electrons stuck in it.	alpha scattering experiment
	Nuclear model — positively charged nucleus surrounded by cloud of negative electrons.	Niels Bohr's theoretical calculations (that agreed with experimental data).
	Bohr model — electrons orbit the nucleus at certain distances.	

alpha particles   gold foil

a few deflected back   most passed through

Experiment showed:

kg Most of the mass of an atom is concentrated at the centre (nucleus).

+ Nucleus is positively charged.

It was discovered the nucleus could be split into smaller particles. ➡ First, the positive proton was found. ➡

About 20 years after the idea of the nucleus was accepted, James Chadwick proved neutrons exist.

The Current Model of the Atom

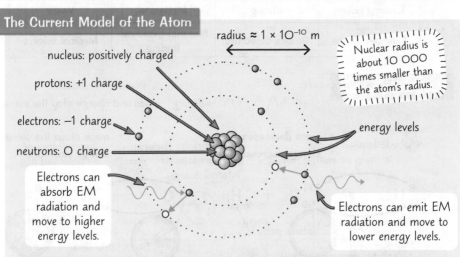

radius ≈ 1×10^{-10} m

Nuclear radius is about 10 000 times smaller than the atom's radius.

nucleus: positively charged

protons: +1 charge

electrons: −1 charge

neutrons: 0 charge

energy levels

Electrons can absorb EM radiation and move to higher energy levels.

Electrons can emit EM radiation and move to lower energy levels.

An atom's overall electric charge is zero: number of electrons = number of protons.

Isotopes and Nuclear Radiation

Mass Number and Atomic Number

ISOTOPES of an element — atoms with the same number of protons but different numbers of neutrons.

All atoms of each element have a set number of protons.

 MASS NUMBER — total number of protons and neutrons in an atom.

$$^{16}_{8}O$$

ATOMIC NUMBER — number of protons in an atom (equal to charge of nucleus).

Types of Nuclear Radiation

RADIOACTIVE DECAY — when an unstable nucleus decays into another element and gives out radiation to become more stable.

Unstable nuclei can also release neutrons (n) when they decay.

IONISING RADIATION (α, β and γ) — radiation that knocks electrons off atoms, creating positive ions.

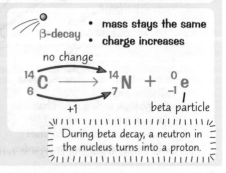

	alpha (α)	beta (β)	gamma (γ)
Consists of...	2 neutrons and 2 protons (helium nucleus)	fast-moving electron from nucleus	electromagnetic radiation from nucleus
Absorbed by...	Sheet of paper	Sheet of aluminium	Thick sheets of lead
Range in air	Few centimetres	Few metres	Longer distances
Ionising power	Strong	Moderate	Weak
Example of use	Smoke detectors	Material thickness testing	Medical tracers

Nuclear Equations

γ-decay   mass and charge stay the same

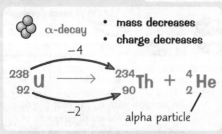

α-decay
• mass decreases
• charge decreases

$$^{238}_{92}U \longrightarrow \, ^{234}_{90}Th + \, ^{4}_{2}He$$
-4
-2
alpha particle

β-decay
• mass stays the same
• charge increases

no change

$$^{14}_{6}C \longrightarrow \, ^{14}_{7}N + \, ^{0}_{-1}e$$
$+1$
beta particle

During beta decay, a neutron in the nucleus turns into a proton.

You don't need to know these particular equations, just how mass and atomic numbers change during decays.

Radioactivity and Risk

Activity and Count-Rate

ACTIVITY — the rate at which a source decays, measured in becquerels (Bq).

COUNT-RATE — the number of radiation counts reaching a detector per second.

A Geiger-Muller tube and counter measure count-rate.

Contamination and Irradiation

RADIOACTIVE CONTAMINATION — getting unwanted radioactive atoms onto or into an object.

IRRADIATION — the exposure of an object to nuclear radiation (doesn't make the object radioactive).

Three precautions to protect against irradiation:

1 Keep sources in lead-lined boxes.

2 Stand behind barriers or be in a different room to the source.

3 Handle sources with remote-controlled arms.

Half-life

Radioactive decay is random.

HALF-LIFE — time taken for the number of nuclei of an isotope in a sample to halve.

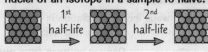

1st half-life → 2nd half-life →

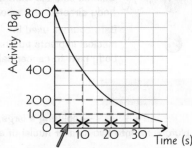

One half-life is the time taken for the activity or count-rate of a sample to halve.

Risk of Radiation

cell can be damaged

damaged cell can multiply and become cancer

radiation can enter a living cell, ionising atoms within it

cell can be killed

Inside body:
- α is most dangerous
- γ is least dangerous

Outside body:
- γ is most dangerous
- α is least dangerous

- An isotope with a short half-life decays quickly — emits high amounts of radiation to start with but quickly becomes safer.

- An isotope with a long half-life decays slowly — emits small amounts of radiation for a long time, so nearby areas are exposed for a long time.

Topic 4 — Atomic Structure

Background Radiation and Uses

Background Radiation

BACKGROUND RADIATION — low-level radiation that's always around us.

Two types of sources:

1 Natural sources — rocks, food, cosmic rays, air, building materials.

2 Man-made sources — nuclear waste, fallout from nuclear explosions.

Radiation Dose

RADIATION DOSE — measure of the risk of harm to body tissues due to exposure to radiation.

Depends on:
- your job
- your location

Medical Uses

Two ways ionising radiation is used in radiotherapy to kill cancer cells:

1 Gamma sources from outside body directed at cancer cells.

2 Beta sources used in medical implants put inside body next to cancer cells.

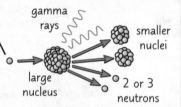

Medical tracer (radioactive source) injected into patient to explore internal organs.

Radiation detected outside the body.

Gamma sources used so that radiation passes out of body.

Nuclear Fission

NUCLEAR FISSION — splitting a large, unstable nucleus (e.g. uranium or plutonium) into two smaller nuclei of approximately the same size.

Fission usually occurs after an unstable nucleus absorbs a neutron. (Spontaneous fission rarely happens.)

gamma rays

smaller nuclei

large nucleus

2 or 3 neutrons

Energy released as gamma rays and in kinetic energy stores of fission products.

Released neutrons can be absorbed by another nucleus, starting a chain reaction...

... controlled in nuclear reactor.

... uncontrolled in nuclear explosion.

Nuclear Fusion

NUCLEAR FUSION — two light nuclei collide at high speed and join to create a larger, heavier nucleus.

lighter nuclei

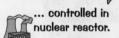

heavier nucleus

Some of the mass of the lighter nuclei is converted into energy, which can be released as radiation.

Scalars, Vectors, Forces and Weight

Scalars

SCALAR QUANTITIES — only have magnitude and no direction.

- speed
- distance
- temperature
- mass
- time

Vectors

VECTOR QUANTITIES — have a magnitude and a direction.

- force
- velocity
- displacement
- acceleration
- momentum

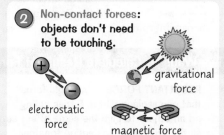

Direction of arrow shows direction of quantity.
Length of arrow shows magnitude.

Forces

FORCE — a push or a pull on an object caused by it interacting with something.

Two types of forces:

1 Contact forces: **objects have to be touching.**

friction   tension

air resistance   normal contact force

2 Non-contact forces: **objects don't need to be touching.**

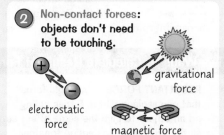

electrostatic force   gravitational force

magnetic force

Weight, Mass and Gravity

WEIGHT — force that acts on an object due to gravity.

Near Earth, weight is caused by gravitational field around Earth.

weight (N)   gravitational field strength (N/kg)

$$W = mg$$

mass (kg)

Weight and mass are directly proportional: $W \propto m$.

Measure weight with calibrated spring-balance (newtonmeter).

CENTRE OF MASS — point at which an object's weight appears to act.

- Object weight depends on strength of gravitational field at object location.
- Object mass has same value anywhere in the universe.

Calculating Forces and Work Done

Free Body Diagrams

FREE BODY DIAGRAM — shows all forces acting on an isolated object.

drag

weight

Arrows show relative magnitudes and directions of forces acting.

Resolving Forces

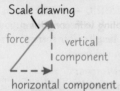

Scale drawing

force

vertical component

horizontal component

Component forces acting together have same effect as the single force.

Equilibrium

EQUILIBRIUM — when the forces acting on an object are balanced and the resultant force is zero.

Object in equilibrium

F_1

F_3

F_2

Drawing forces tip-to-tail in scale drawing creates a closed loop.

F_2

F_1

F_3

Two Ways to Calculate Resultant Force

RESULTANT FORCE — a single force that can replace all the forces acting on an object to give the same effect as all the original forces acting together.

1 Add forces pointing in same direction. Subtract forces pointing in opposite directions.

F_1 F_2

$F_1 - F_2$ = resultant force

2 Draw forces to scale and tip-to-tail.

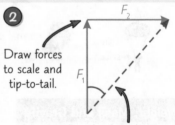

F_2

F_1

Measure length of resultant force to find its magnitude, and angle to find its direction.

Work Done

When a force moves an object from one point to another, energy is transferred and work is done on the object.

work done (J)
(1 joule = 1 newton metre)

force (N)

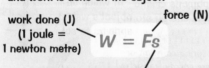

$$W = Fs$$

distance (moved along the line of action of the force) (m)

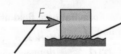

Box does work against frictional forces causing temperature of box to increase.

Force does work on box and energy is transferred to box's kinetic energy store.

Forces and Elasticity

Changing Shape

More than one force has to act on a stationary object to change its shape.

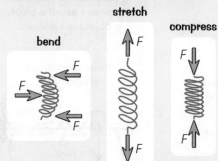

bend

stretch

compress

Two Types of Deformation

1 ELASTIC — object goes back to its original shape and length after forces have been removed.

Elastic objects can be elastically deformed, e.g. a spring.

2 INELASTIC — object doesn't go back to its original shape and length after forces have been removed.

Force-Extension Relationship for an Elastic Object

force (N)

extension or compression (m)

$$F = ke$$

spring constant (N/m)

Extension of a stretched spring is directly proportional to load or force applied. Graph is linear.

limit of proportionality

Force gets too big — extension no longer proportional to force. Graph is non-linear.

Work Done and Elasticity

Force stretches or compresses object. ➡ Work is done. ➡ Energy transferred to object's elastic potential energy store.

I always like to spend the morning getting some work done.

In elastic deformation, all energy is transferred to object's elastic potential energy store.

The larger the spring constant or extension, the more energy transferred to object's elastic potential energy store.

Moments

Calculating Moments

MOMENT — the turning effect of a force.

moment of a
force (Nm) ⟋   force (N)

$$M = Fd$$

perpendicular distance from the pivot
to the line of action of the force (m)

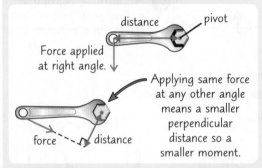

distance   pivot

Force applied
at right angle. ↓

force ---↴ distance

Applying same force
at any other angle
means a smaller
perpendicular
distance so a
smaller moment.

Balanced Moments

If total clockwise moment
equals total anticlockwise
moment about a pivot,
object is balanced.

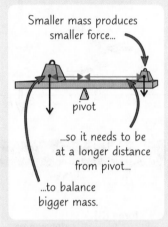

Smaller mass produces
smaller force...

pivot

...so it needs to be
at a longer distance
from pivot...

...to balance
bigger mass.

Gears

GEARS — used to transmit
the rotational effect of a force
from one place to another.

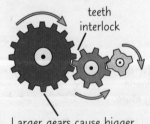

teeth
interlock

Larger gears cause bigger
moments but turn more slowly.

Levers

LEVERS — make it easier
to do work e.g. lift a load.

If only levers
made doing
revision easier...

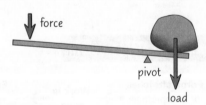

force

pivot

load

Increasing
distance
between pivot
and applied force → Less force
required to
get the same
moment → Easier to
lift load

Fluid Pressure and Upthrust

Calculating Pressure

Pressure of a fluid means a force is exerted normal to any surface in contact with the fluid.

A fluid is either a liquid or a gas.

pressure (Pa)

$$p = \frac{F}{A}$$

area of that surface (m²)

force normal to a surface (N)

Pressure Differences in a Liquid

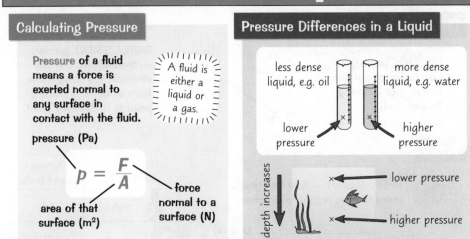

less dense liquid, e.g. oil

more dense liquid, e.g. water

lower pressure

higher pressure

depth increases

lower pressure

higher pressure

Upthrust

UPTHRUST — the resultant force acting upwards on an object submerged in liquid, due to the pressure of the liquid being greater at the bottom of the object than at the top.

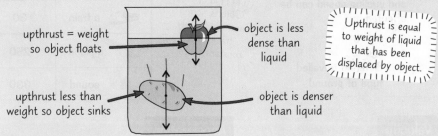

upthrust = weight so object floats

object is less dense than liquid

Upthrust is equal to weight of liquid that has been displaced by object.

upthrust less than weight so object sinks

object is denser than liquid

Atmospheric Pressure

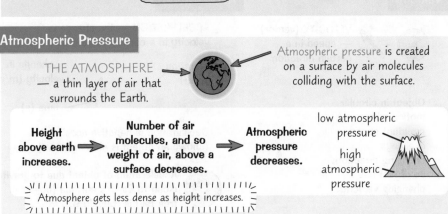

THE ATMOSPHERE — a thin layer of air that surrounds the Earth.

Atmospheric pressure is created on a surface by air molecules colliding with the surface.

Height above earth increases. ➡ Number of air molecules, and so weight of air, above a surface decreases. ➡ Atmospheric pressure decreases.

low atmospheric pressure

high atmospheric pressure

Atmosphere gets less dense as height increases.

Topic 5 — Forces

Motion

Distance and Displacement

DISTANCE (scalar) — how far an object has moved (not including its direction).

finish

DISPLACEMENT (vector) — the distance and the direction in a straight line from an object's starting point to its finishing point.

start

Speed

SPEED (scalar) — how fast you're going with no regard to direction.

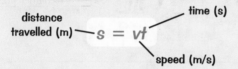

distance travelled (m) — $s = vt$ — time (s)

speed (m/s)

People's walking, running and cycling speed can be affected by:

- ability
- age
- distance travelled
- type of ground

Objects, sound and wind rarely travel at a constant speed.

		Typical speed (m/s)
	walking	1.5
	running	3
	cycling	6
	a car	25
	a train	30
	a plane	250
	sound	330

Velocity

 +

VELOCITY (vector) — speed in a certain direction.

Object in circular motion with constant speed is always changing direction, so object has changing velocity.

Acceleration

ACCELERATION — the change in velocity in a certain amount of time.

acceleration (m/s²)

$$a = \frac{\Delta v}{t}$$

change in velocity (m/s)

time (s)

Deceleration is negative acceleration (shows an object is slowing down).

 Acceleration of object due to gravity close to Earth's surface (object in free fall) is roughly 9.8 m/s².

Distance-Time & Velocity-Time Graphs

Distance-Time Graphs

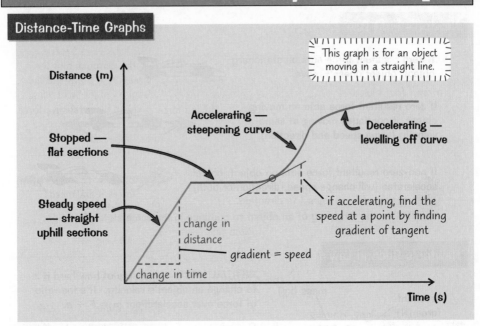

Distance (m)

This graph is for an object moving in a straight line.

Accelerating — steepening curve

Decelerating — levelling off curve

Stopped — flat sections

Steady speed — straight uphill sections

change in distance

gradient = speed

change in time

if accelerating, find the speed at a point by finding gradient of tangent

Time (s)

Velocity-Time Graphs

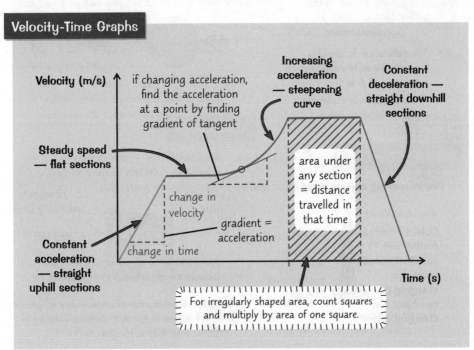

Velocity (m/s)

if changing acceleration, find the acceleration at a point by finding gradient of tangent

Increasing acceleration — steepening curve

Constant deceleration — straight downhill sections

Steady speed — flat sections

change in velocity

gradient = acceleration

change in time

area under any section = distance travelled in that time

Constant acceleration — straight uphill sections

Time (s)

For irregularly shaped area, count squares and multiply by area of one square.

Topic 5 — Forces

Newton's Laws of Motion

Newton's First Law

If zero resultant force acts on stationary object, object doesn't move.

If zero resultant force acts on moving object, it continues moving at same velocity (same speed and direction).

driving force   resistive force
forces balanced

If non-zero resultant force acts on object, object accelerates (will change speed, direction or both).

forces unbalanced

INERTIA — the tendency of an object to continue in the same state of motion.

Newton's Second Law

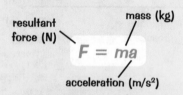
resultant force (N)   mass (kg)
$$F = ma$$
acceleration (m/s^2)

- **Acceleration is directly proportional to resultant force — $F \propto a$.**
- **Acceleration is inversely proportional to mass.**

INERTIAL MASS — measure of how hard it is to change an object's velocity. It's the ratio of force over acceleration: $m = F \div a$.

Same force applied to bowling ball and golf ball.

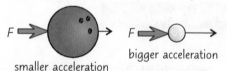
F F
smaller acceleration   bigger acceleration

Bowling ball has bigger inertial mass, so it's harder to increase its velocity.

Newton's Third Law

Two interacting objects exert equal and opposite forces on each other.

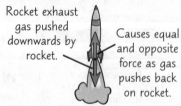
Rocket exhaust gas pushed downwards by rocket.

Causes equal and opposite force as gas pushes back on rocket.

Rocket moves when upwards force is greater than rocket's weight.

Girl pushes on wall.

Equilibrium — wall pushes back on girl with equal and opposite force.

You don't need to learn these specific examples, but you need to know how to apply Newton's third law to different situations.

Terminal Velocity and Reaction Times

Terminal Velocity

FRICTION — a force that acts to oppose an object's motion. It always acts in the opposite direction to movement.

DRAG — the frictional force caused by any fluid on a moving object (e.g. air resistance).

Frictional forces from fluids always increase with speed.

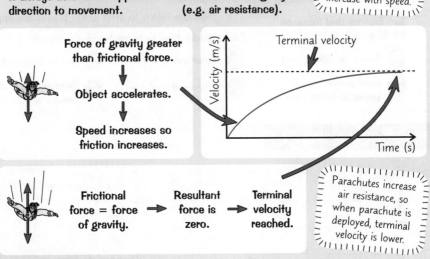

Force of gravity greater than frictional force.

↓

Object accelerates.

↓

Speed increases so friction increases.

Terminal velocity

Velocity (m/s)

Time (s)

Frictional force = force of gravity. → Resultant force is zero. → Terminal velocity reached.

Parachutes increase air resistance, so when parachute is deployed, terminal velocity is lower.

Reaction Times

Typical reaction time: between 0.2 and 0.9 s.

Three factors affecting reaction times:

Distractions affect your ability to react.

1 Tiredness **2** Drugs **3** Alcohol

The Ruler Drop Test

Three steps to investigate reaction time:

1 Get someone to hold ruler so zero is between your thumb and forefinger.

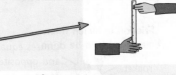

2 Ruler dropped without warning. Catch it as quickly as possible.

3 Use distance ruler fell to calculate reaction time.

distance fallen

The longer the distance, the longer the reaction time.

Topic 5 — Forces

Stopping Distances

Stopping Distance Equation

Stopping distance = Thinking distance + Braking distance

How far vehicle moves during driver's reaction time.

Distance taken to stop whilst brakes are applied.

Two factors that increase thinking distance:

1 faster vehicle speed

2 slow driver reaction times

Four factors that increase braking distance:

1 faster vehicle speed

2 wet or icy weather

3 poor road surface

4 damaged or worn brakes or tyres

Stopping Distance Graphs

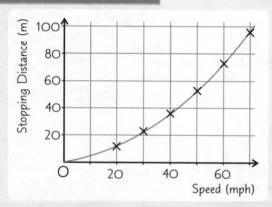

Speed (mph)

The bigger the stopping distance, the more space drivers need to leave between their car and the one in front.

If speed doubles:
- thinking distance doubles
- braking distance quadruples

Work Done When Stopping

Driver brakes, causing brake pads to be pressed onto wheels.

⬇

Friction between them causes work to be done.

⬇

Energy transferred from kinetic energy stores of wheels to thermal energy stores of brakes.

⬇

Brakes heat up.

Large Decelerations

The faster a vehicle is going, the greater the braking force needed to make it stop in a certain distance.

⬇

Larger braking force means larger deceleration.

Very large deceleration can cause:

 brakes to overheat

 vehicle to skid

Momentum

Calculating Momentum

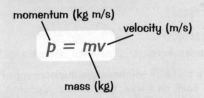

momentum (kg m/s)

velocity (m/s)

$$p = mv$$

mass (kg)

The greater an object's mass, the greater its momentum.

The greater an object's velocity, the greater its momentum.

Conservation of Momentum

CONSERVATION OF MOMENTUM — in a closed system, total momentum before an event (e.g. a collision) equals total momentum after an event.

Before explosion, momentum is zero.

After explosion, pieces fly off in different directions so momentum cancels out to zero.

Forces, Momentum and Safety

The resultant force acting on an object is equal to its rate of change in momentum.

Increasing time taken for momentum to change decreases force acting on object.

Five safety features that increase time for change in momentum:

① Air bags

② Seat belts

③ Cushioned playground flooring

④ Crash mats

⑤ Bike helmets

Air bag inflates during car crash.

Compressing air decreases your velocity over a longer time compared to hitting the dashboard.

Rate of change of momentum is smaller.

Forces felt are smaller (meaning less severe injuries).

Transverse and Longitudinal Waves

Wave Basics

When waves travel through a medium, they transfer energy (and not matter).

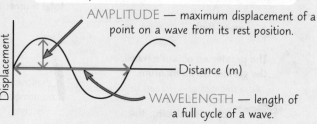

Sound waves move away...

...the air particles don't.

Ripples on water's surface move away...

...the water doesn't.

FREQUENCY — number of complete waves passing a certain point each second.

PERIOD — amount of time it takes for a complete wave to pass a point.

AMPLITUDE — maximum displacement of a point on a wave from its rest position.

Displacement

Distance (m)

WAVELENGTH — length of a full cycle of a wave.

When a wave hits a boundary, it can be absorbed, transmitted or reflected.

Transverse Waves

Oscillations perpendicular (at 90°) to direction of energy transfer.

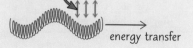

energy transfer

Three types of transverse waves:

1. Ripples in water

2. Electromagnetic waves (e.g. light)

3. Waves on a string

Longitudinal Waves

Oscillations parallel to direction of energy transfer.

compressions

rarefactions

energy transfer

Two types of longitudinal waves:

1. Sound waves

2. P-waves

The Wave Equation

WAVE SPEED — speed at which a wave transfers energy (or speed the wave moves at).

frequency (hertz, Hz)

wave speed (m/s)

$$v = f\lambda$$

wavelength (m)

1 Hz is 1 wave per second.

Speed of Sound and Reflection

Measuring the Speed of Sound

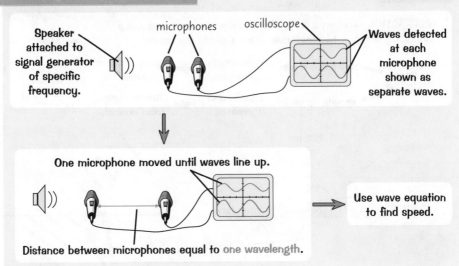

Speaker attached to signal generator of specific frequency.

microphones

oscilloscope

Waves detected at each microphone shown as separate waves.

One microphone moved until waves line up.

Use wave equation to find speed.

Distance between microphones equal to one wavelength.

Reflection

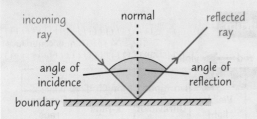

incoming ray

normal

reflected ray

angle of incidence

angle of reflection

boundary

Angle of incidence always equals angle of reflection.

Angel of reflection.

Diffuse Reflection

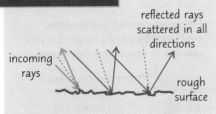

reflected rays scattered in all directions

incoming rays

rough surface

Surface appears matte (e.g. piece of paper).

Specular Reflection

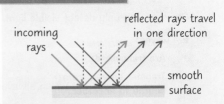

incoming rays

reflected rays travel in one direction

smooth surface

Surface gives clear reflection (e.g. mirror).

Topic 6 — Waves

Refraction and EM Waves

Refraction

REFRACTION — when a wave changes direction as it crosses a
boundary between two materials at an angle to the normal.

Wave
refracts
- slows down ⟹ Wavelength decreases. ⟹ Bends towards normal.
- speeds up ⟹ Wavelength increases. ⟹ Bends away from normal.

Frequency
never changes.

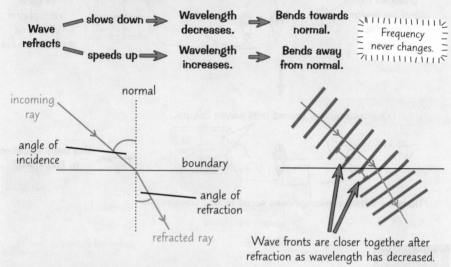

Wave fronts are closer together after
refraction as wavelength has decreased.

The Electromagnetic (EM) Spectrum

The EM spectrum is continuous.

red ⟶ violet

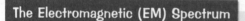

Radio waves	Microwaves	Infrared	Visible light	Ultraviolet	X-rays	Gamma rays

Increasing frequency, decreasing wavelength

Our eyes can only detect visible light.

EM waves:

- Are transverse.

- Transfer energy from
  source to absorber.

- Travel at same speed
  in air or vacuum.

EM waves created and absorbed
over large frequency range due to
changes in atoms and their nuclei.

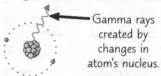

Gamma rays
created by
changes in
atom's nucleus.

Uses and Dangers of EM Waves

Producing Radio Waves

Electrons oscillate, producing radio waves.

Alternating current supplied (shown on an oscilloscope).

transmitter

receiver

Radio waves absorbed, causing electrons in receiver to oscillate.

Emitted radio waves transfer energy.

Alternating current of same frequency as radio waves induced in receiver.

Uses of EM Waves

Radio waves

- **TV**
- **Radio**

Microwaves

- **Satellite communications**
- **Cooking**

Infrared radiation

- **Electric heaters**
- **Cooking**
- **Infrared cameras**

Visible light

- **Communications through optical fibres**

UV waves

- **Energy efficient lights**
- **Sun tan beds**

X-rays and gamma rays

- **Medical imaging**
- **Medical treatments**

Dangers of EM Waves

RADIATION DOSE — measure of the risk of harm to body tissues due to exposure to radiation. It is measured in sieverts.

1 sievert (Sv) = 1000 millisieverts (mSv).

Risk depends on:
- Size of dose
- Type of radiation

Type of ionising radiation	UV	X-rays and gamma rays
Harmful effects on human body tissue	• Can prematurely age skin • Increases risk of skin cancer	• Gene mutation • Cancer

Lenses and Magnification

Images

REAL IMAGE	image formed when light rays from a point on an object come together at another point
VIRTUAL IMAGE	image formed when light rays appear to have come from one point, but have actually come from another

Lenses form images by refracting light.

Convex Lenses

Convex lenses can produce real or virtual images.

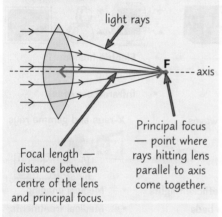

light rays

F ---- axis

Focal length — distance between centre of the lens and principal focus.

Principal focus — point where rays hitting lens parallel to axis come together.

Concave Lenses

Concave lenses always produce virtual images.

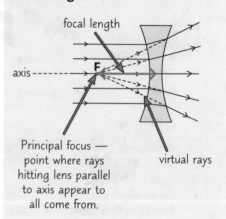

focal length

axis ----- F

Principal focus — point where rays hitting lens parallel to axis appear to all come from.

virtual rays

Magnifying Glasses

This is one convex investigation...

Magnifying glasses use convex lenses to create a virtual image.

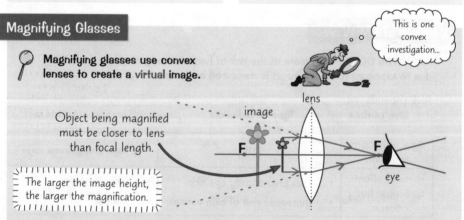

Object being magnified must be closer to lens than focal length.

image

lens

F   F

eye

The larger the image height, the larger the magnification.

Ray Diagrams

Four Ray Diagrams for Convex Lenses

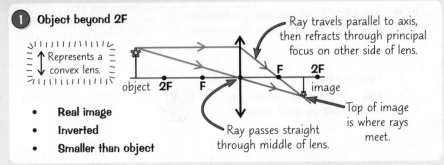

1 Object beyond 2F

Represents a convex lens.

Ray travels parallel to axis, then refracts through principal focus on other side of lens.

object 2F F F 2F image

Top of image is where rays meet.

Ray passes straight through middle of lens.

- **Real image**
- **Inverted**
- **Smaller than object**

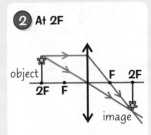

2 At 2F

object 2F F F 2F image

- **Real image**
- **Inverted**
- **Same size as object**

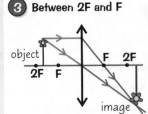

3 Between 2F and F

object 2F F F 2F image

- **Real image**
- **Inverted**
- **Bigger than object**

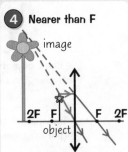

4 Nearer than F

image

2F F object F 2F

- **Virtual image**
- **Upright**
- **Bigger than object**

Ray Diagram for Concave Lenses

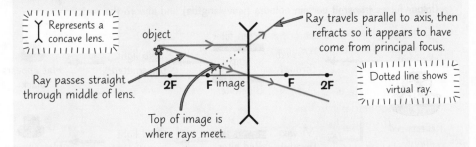

Represents a concave lens.

object

Ray travels parallel to axis, then refracts so it appears to have come from principal focus.

Ray passes straight through middle of lens.

2F F image F 2F

Dotted line shows virtual ray.

Top of image is where rays meet.

- **Virtual image**
- **Upright**
- **Smaller than object**

Visible Light

Colour

In the visible light spectrum, every colour has a small range of wavelengths (and frequencies).

White light is made up of all colours.

- Opaque objects don't transmit light.
- Colour depends on wavelengths of light that are most reflected.

red apple

All other wavelengths are absorbed.

Black objects absorb all wavelengths of visible light.

White objects reflect all wavelengths of visible light equally.

- Transparent (see-through) or translucent (partially see-through) objects transmit light.
- Colour depends on wavelengths of light it transmits and reflects.

white

Colour Filters

Colour filters transmit certain colours (wavelengths) and absorb the rest.

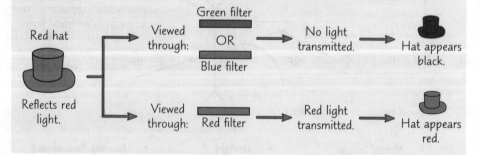

Red hat

Reflects red light.

Viewed through:

Green filter

OR

Blue filter

No light transmitted.

Hat appears black.

Viewed through: Red filter

Red light transmitted.

Hat appears red.

Emitting and Absorbing Radiation

Infrared Radiation

All objects continually emit and absorb infrared (IR) radiation.

Tree and surroundings are at same temperature...

... so tree absorbs IR radiation at the same rate it emits it...

... which keeps it at constant temperature.

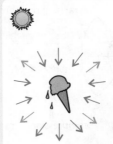

Ice cream colder than surroundings...

... so it absorbs IR radiation faster than it emits it...

... which increases its temperature.

Black Bodies

PERFECT BLACK BODY — an object that absorbs all radiation that hits it.

Two properties of perfect black bodies:

1. Best possible emitters of radiation.

2. Don't reflect or transmit any radiation.

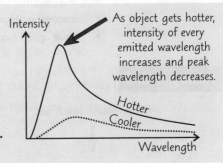

Intensity

As object gets hotter, intensity of every emitted wavelength increases and peak wavelength decreases.

Hotter

Cooler

Wavelength

Radiation and Earth's Temperature

Daytime: Earth absorbs more radiation than it emits.

Local temperature increases.

Nighttime: Earth emits more radiation than it absorbs.

Local temperature decreases.

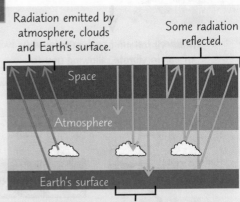

Radiation emitted by atmosphere, clouds and Earth's surface.

Some radiation reflected.

Space

Atmosphere

Earth's surface

Some radiation from Sun absorbed by atmosphere, clouds and Earth's surface.

Topic 6 — Waves

Sound Waves

Vibrations

Vibrating object (loudspeaker) creates sound waves.

Sound wave travels as series of compressions and rarefactions through air.

Sound waves hitting solid causes particles in solid to vibrate.

solid object

Particles hit next particles in line and so on — sound wave travels through solid as series of vibrations.

compression   rarefaction

When a sound wave enters denser material:
- **wavelength increases**
- **frequency stays the same**
- **wave speed increases**

Hearing Sound

Sound waves reach ear.

↓

Cause ear drum to vibrate.

↓

These vibrations cause other parts of ear to vibrate, allowing you to hear the sound waves.

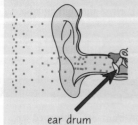

ear drum

ear drum and bass

Human Hearing

Conversion of sound waves to vibrations at ear drum only works over a certain frequency range.

Three factors that limit frequency range:

1. Size of ear drum.

2. Shape of ear drum.

3. Structure of all parts within the ear that vibrate.

Normal human hearing range:

20 Hz – 20 kHz

Uses of Sound Waves

Ultrasound

ULTRASOUND — sound waves with frequencies higher than 20 kHz.

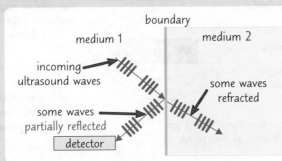

boundary

medium 1   medium 2

incoming ultrasound waves

some waves refracted

some waves partially reflected

detector

 Time it takes ultrasound waves to be partially reflected back from boundary and reach detector can be used to measure distance to boundary.

Three uses of ultrasound:

1
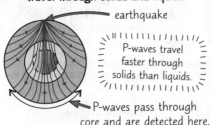
Medical imaging, e.g. pre-natal scanning of foetus.

2

Industrial imaging, e.g. finding flaws in materials.

3
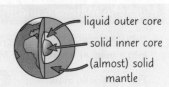
Echo sounding, e.g. finding depth of water or locating objects in deep water.

Seismic Waves

Earthquakes produce seismic waves.

Detecting seismic waves gives evidence for size of Earth's core and Earth's structure:

liquid outer core
solid inner core
(almost) solid mantle

P-waves
- Longitudinal waves.
- Travel through solids and liquids.

earthquake

P-waves travel faster through solids than liquids.

P-waves pass through core and are detected here.

S-waves
- Transverse waves.
- Can't travel through liquids.

earthquake

S-waves don't pass through core and aren't detected here.

Magnets

Magnetic Fields

PERMANENT MAGNET — produces its own magnetic field.

Magnetic field is strongest at the poles.

Magnetic field strength decreases with distance from magnet.

Field lines show direction force would act on a north pole, if placed at that point.

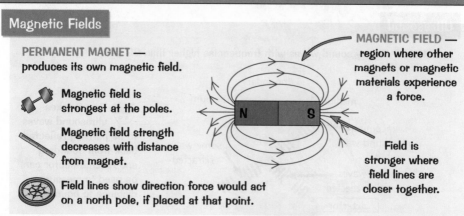

MAGNETIC FIELD — region where other magnets or magnetic materials experience a force.

Field is stronger where field lines are closer together.

Repulsion

Like poles repel.

Attraction

Unlike poles attract.

Forces between magnets are non-contact forces.

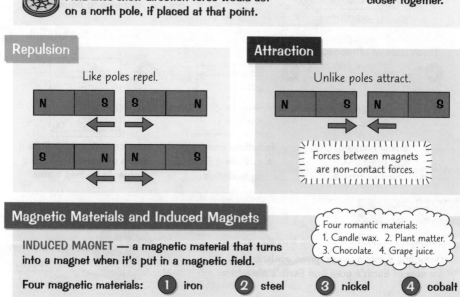

Magnetic Materials and Induced Magnets

INDUCED MAGNET — a magnetic material that turns into a magnet when it's put in a magnetic field.

Four romantic materials:
1. Candle wax. 2. Plant matter.
3. Chocolate. 4. Grape juice.

Four magnetic materials:　**1** iron　**2** steel　**3** nickel　**4** cobalt

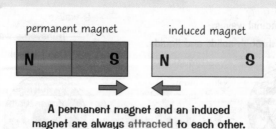

permanent magnet　　　induced magnet

A permanent magnet and an induced magnet are always attracted to each other.

When the induced magnet is moved away from the permanent magnet, it quickly loses all (or most) of its magnetism.

Compasses and Electromagnetism

Compasses

Compass needle points in the direction of the magnetic field it's in.

A compass needle is a small bar magnet.

 When a compass isn't near a magnet, its needle points north to line up with the Earth's magnetic field.

Current-Carrying Wire

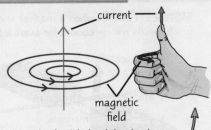

current

magnetic field

Use the right-hand thumb rule to work out the direction of a magnetic field around a current-carrying wire.

Two factors the magnetic field strength depends on:

1 Size of current.

2 Distance from the wire.

Solenoids and Magnetic Fields

Twisting a wire into a solenoid increases the magnetic field strength around the wire.

Magnetic fields of each turn of wire add together. So magnetic field inside solenoid is strong and uniform.

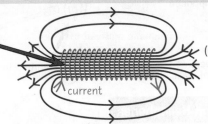

current

magnetic field (same shape as a bar magnet)

ELECTROMAGNET — a solenoid with an iron core. It is a magnet that can be turned on and off.

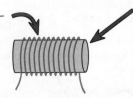

Putting an iron core in a solenoid increases its magnetic field strength.

Electromagnets are used in fire alarm bells and in scrap yards to pick up large objects.

Topic 7 — Magnetism and Electromagnetism

The Motor Effect

Force on a Conductor

MOTOR EFFECT — when a magnet and a current-carrying conductor exert a force on each other.

Fleming's left-hand rule.

force

magnetic field

force

magnetic field

N S

current through conductor

magnetic field

current

Three ways to increase the force:

1. increase the current

2. increase the magnetic field strength

3. increase the length of the conductor

Electric Motors

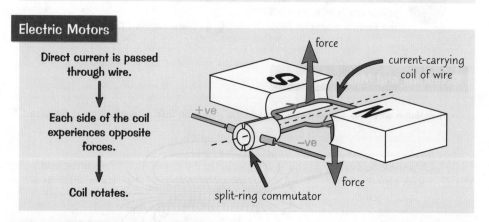

Direct current is passed through wire.

↓

Each side of the coil experiences opposite forces.

↓

Coil rotates.

force

current-carrying coil of wire

S

N

+ve

−ve

force

split-ring commutator

Loudspeakers and Headphones

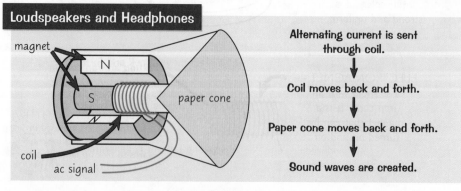

magnet

N

S

paper cone

coil

ac signal

Alternating current is sent through coil.

↓

Coil moves back and forth.

↓

Paper cone moves back and forth.

↓

Sound waves are created.

Topic 7 — Magnetism and Electromagnetism

The Generator Effect and Microphones

The Generator Effect

GENERATOR EFFECT — when a potential difference is induced in a wire which is moving relative to a magnetic field, or experiencing a change in magnetic field.

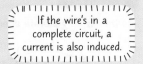
If the wire's in a complete circuit, a current is also induced.

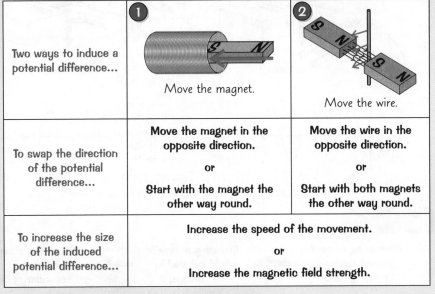

	1	**2**
Two ways to induce a potential difference...	Move the magnet.	Move the wire.
To swap the direction of the potential difference...	Move the magnet in the opposite direction. or Start with the magnet the other way round.	Move the wire in the opposite direction. or Start with both magnets the other way round.
To increase the size of the induced potential difference...	Increase the speed of the movement. or Increase the magnetic field strength.	

An induced current generates its own magnetic field.

An induced current generates a magnetic field that always acts against the change that made it.

Microphones

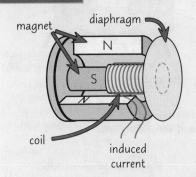

magnet
diaphragm
N
S
coil
induced current

Sound waves hit diaphragm.

↓

Diaphragm moves back and forth.

↓

Coil of wire moves back and forth.

↓

Alternating current is generated.

Generators and Transformers

Alternators

Alternators **generate alternating current.**

force applied

slip rings
and brushes

induced ac

potential
difference

time

Dynamos

Dynamos **generate direct current.**

force applied

split-ring
commutator

induced dc

potential
difference

time

Peak height will increase if speed of coil increases.

Transformers

**Alternating current
passed through
primary coil.** ⟹ **Changing magnetic
field induced in
iron core.** ⟹ **Alternating current
induced in
secondary coil.**

Step-up **transformer**
$V_P < V_S$

iron core
(easily magnetised)

primary coil
(fewer turns)

secondary coil
(more turns)

Step-down **transformer**
$V_P > V_S$

magnetic
field

primary coil
(more turns)

secondary coil
(fewer turns)

Changing the
number of
turns on a coil
changes the
output potential
difference.

**ratio between primary and secondary potential differences
= ratio between number of turns on primary and secondary coils**

If transformer is 100% efficient: input power = output power.

Stars and the Solar System

The Life Cycle of a Star

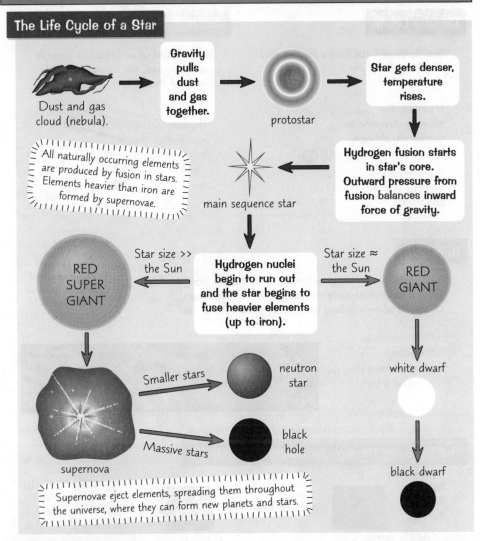

Dust and gas cloud (nebula).

Gravity pulls dust and gas together.

protostar

Star gets denser, temperature rises.

Hydrogen fusion starts in star's core. Outward pressure from fusion balances inward force of gravity.

All naturally occurring elements are produced by fusion in stars. Elements heavier than iron are formed by supernovae.

main sequence star

Hydrogen nuclei begin to run out and the star begins to fuse heavier elements (up to iron).

Star size >> the Sun

RED SUPER GIANT

Star size ≈ the Sun

RED GIANT

Smaller stars → neutron star

Massive stars → black hole

supernova

white dwarf

black dwarf

Supernovae eject elements, spreading them throughout the universe, where they can form new planets and stars.

Our Solar System

- Our solar system is a tiny part of the **Milky Way galaxy**.
- It contains the **Sun**, **eight planets**, **dwarf planets**, **moons** (natural satellites) and **artificial satellites**.
- **Planets orbit the Sun**, moons orbit planets and artificial satellites (generally) orbit the Earth.

Artificial satellites are man-made, natural satellites aren't.

Orbits, Red-Shift and The Big Bang

Circular Orbits

Gravitational force keeps planets and satellites in circular orbits.

It causes the object's direction to constantly change.

This means the object's velocity constantly changes.

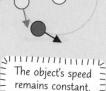

The object's speed remains constant.

Stable Orbits

If the speed of an object in a stable orbit changes, the radius (size) of the orbit changes.

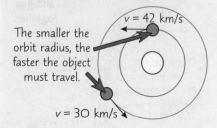

The smaller the orbit radius, the faster the object must travel.

$v = 42$ km/s

$v = 30$ km/s

Red-Shift

RED-SHIFT — an observed increase in the wavelength of light (light is shifted towards the red end of the spectrum). Observed when a galaxy moves away from the Earth.

The light observed from most galaxies is red-shifted.

The more distant the galaxy:

- the faster it moves away from us
- the greater its red-shift

The Big Bang Theory and Universal Mysteries

Big Bang theory:

All the matter in the universe occupied a dense and hot tiny space.

Then it 'exploded' and space started expanding.

Red-shift provides evidence that the whole universe is expanding and so supports the Big Bang theory.

Three things in the universe that aren't fully understood:

1. Why distant galaxies are receding at increasing speeds (shown by observations of supernovae since 1998).

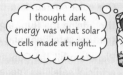

I thought dark energy was what solar cells made at night...

2. Dark matter

3. Dark energy

Required Practicals 1

Specific Heat Capacity

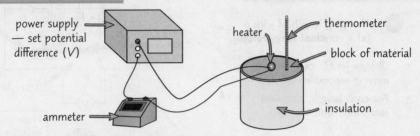

power supply — set potential difference (V)

heater

thermometer

block of material

ammeter

insulation

Six steps to find specific heat capacity of material:

1. Turn on power supply.

2. Measure temperature every minute for 10 minutes.

3. Calculate power with $P = VI$ (I is current).

4. For each minute over the 10 minutes, calculate energy transferred with $E = Pt$ (t is time in seconds).

5. Plot graph. ⟶

6. $$\text{Specific heat capacity} = \frac{1}{\text{gradient} \times \text{mass of block}}$$

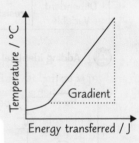

Temperature / °C

Gradient

Energy transferred / J

Thermal Insulators

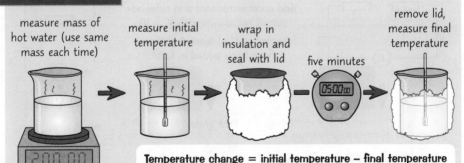

measure mass of hot water (use same mass each time)

measure initial temperature

wrap in insulation and seal with lid

five minutes

05:00:00

remove lid, measure final temperature

200.00

Temperature change = initial temperature − final temperature

Repeat with either different materials or different thicknesses.

The lower the temperature change, the better the thermal insulation.

Independent Variable	Dependent Variable
type of material or material thickness	temperature change

Required Practicals 2

Two Resistance Experiments

① Changing length of wire (at a constant temperature).

- Change length of wire by moving crocodile clip.
- For each length, calculate resistance with $V = IR$.

Independent Variable	length of wire
Dependent Variable	resistance

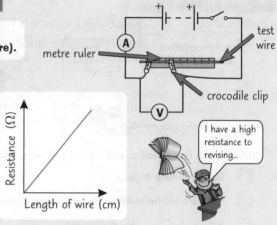

metre ruler

test wire

crocodile clip

I have a high resistance to revising...

Resistance (Ω) vs Length of wire (cm)

② Adding identical resistors in series or parallel.

SERIES

battery with potential difference V

PARALLEL

Calculate resistance of initial circuit with $V = IR$.

Add another resistor and calculate overall resistance with $V = IR$.

Repeat until at least 4 resistors have been added in total.

Plot graph.

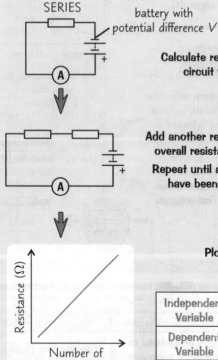

Resistance (Ω) vs Number of identical resistors

Independent Variable	number of resistors
Dependent Variable	resistance

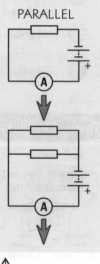

Resistance (Ω) vs Number of identical resistors

Required Practicals 3

I-V Characteristics

Three steps to find a component's *I-V* characteristic:

1 Vary variable resistor to change current through circuit, and then take a reading of *I* and *V*. Repeat several times.

2 Swap over wires connected to battery (so current is reversed) and repeat step 1.

3 Plot values on *I-V* graph.

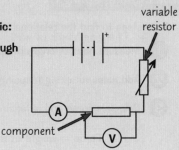

variable resistor

component

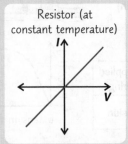

Resistor (at constant temperature)

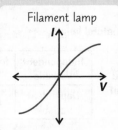

Filament lamp

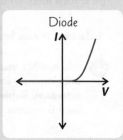

Diode

Determining Density of Solids and Liquids

Use balance to find mass.

Regular solid

Measure with ruler. Calculate volume using relevant formula for shape.

For small dimensions, use vernier callipers or a micrometer.

$$\text{Density} \ (\text{kg/m}^3) = \frac{\text{mass (kg)}}{\text{volume (m}^3)}$$

Irregular solid

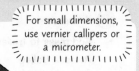

Use eureka can to find volume.

Pour 10 ml of liquid into measuring cylinder on balance.

Record mass and total volume.

Repeat this until measuring cylinder full.

Use the formula for each measurement. Then take an average of calculated densities.

$$\text{Density} \ (\text{kg/m}^3) = \frac{\text{mass (kg)}}{\text{volume (m}^3)}$$

Required Practicals 4

Investigating Springs

Four steps to find the relationship between force and extension:

1 Measure natural length of spring with ruler.

2 Add mass to spring (causing it to extend).

3 Calculate force and extension:

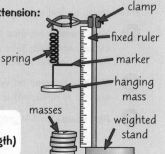

clamp

fixed ruler

spring

marker

hanging mass

masses

weighted stand

> Force = weight of masses = mg
> (m is total mass on spring, g is gravitational field strength)

> Extension = new length − natural length

4 Add another mass and calculate new force and extension. Repeat for at least 6 masses.

Independent Variable	force applied to spring
Dependent Variable	extension

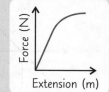

Force (N) vs Extension (m)

Two Experiments that Test $F = ma$

1 Increase mass

- Add mass to trolley.
- Release trolley from starting line. Light gate records trolley's acceleration.
- Add another mass to trolley and repeat until all masses added.

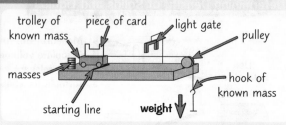

trolley of known mass

piece of card

light gate

pulley

masses

hook of known mass

starting line

weight

Independent Variable	mass
Dependent Variable	acceleration
Control Variable	force (weight)

Increasing mass decreases acceleration.

2 Increase force

- Start with all masses on trolley.
- Move one to hook and release trolley from starting line. Light gate records trolley's acceleration.
- Move another mass to hook and repeat until all masses moved.

Independent Variable	Dependent Variable	Control Variable
force (weight)	acceleration	mass

Increasing force applied increases acceleration.

Required Practicals 5

Two Ways to Measure Wave Speed

① **Waves in a ripple tank.**

Fast wave speed = sore wrist.

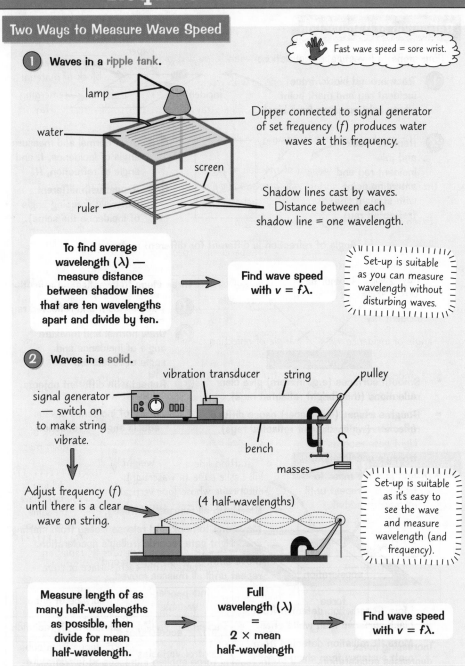

lamp

water

screen

ruler

Dipper connected to signal generator of set frequency (f) produces water waves at this frequency.

Shadow lines cast by waves. Distance between each shadow line = one wavelength.

To find average wavelength (λ) — measure distance between shadow lines that are ten wavelengths apart and divide by ten.

Find wave speed with $v = f\lambda$.

Set-up is suitable as you can measure wavelength without disturbing waves.

② **Waves in a solid.**

vibration transducer   string   pulley

signal generator — switch on to make string vibrate.

bench

masses

Adjust frequency (f) until there is a clear wave on string.

(4 half-wavelengths)

Set-up is suitable as it's easy to see the wave and measure wavelength (and frequency).

Measure length of as many half-wavelengths as possible, then divide for mean half-wavelength.

Full wavelength (λ) = 2 × mean half-wavelength

Find wave speed with $v = f\lambda$.

Required Practicals

Required Practicals 6

Refraction and Reflection

Four steps to investigating refraction:

① Trace around block, trace incident ray and mark point where light emerges from block.

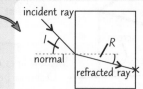

② Remove block and join incident ray and emerging point with straight line (refracted ray).

③ Draw normal and measure angle of incidence, *I*, and angle of refraction, *R*.

④ Repeat with different materials (keeping angle of incidence the same).

Angle of refraction is different for different materials.

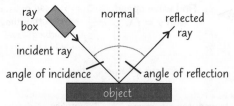

Three steps to investigating reflection:

① Trace incident and reflected ray.

② Draw normal and measure angle of incidence and angle of reflection.

③ Repeat with different objects.

- Smooth surfaces (e.g. mirrors) give clear reflections (thin, bright reflected rays).
- Rough surfaces (e.g. paper) cause diffuse reflection (wider, dimmer reflected rays).

Angle of incidence always equals angle of reflection.

Investigating IR Radiation

Fill Leslie cube (a watertight, metal cube whose four vertical faces have different surfaces) with hot water.

All four surfaces have the same temperature.

IR detector measures IR radiation emitted from each surface of cube.

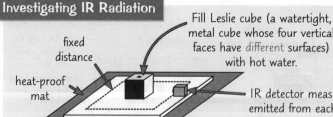

- More IR radiation detected from black surfaces than white ones.
- More IR radiation detected from matt surfaces than shiny ones.

Independent Variable	surface of cube
Dependent Variable	amount of IR radiation
Control Variables	distance from cube and temperature

Apparatus and Techniques

Measuring Length

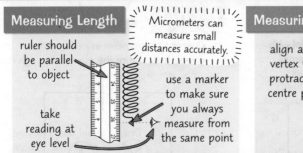

Micrometers can measure small distances accurately.

ruler should be parallel to object

use a marker to make sure you always measure from the same point

take reading at eye level

Measuring Angles

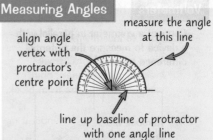

measure the angle at this line

align angle vertex with protractor's centre point

line up baseline of protractor with one angle line

Measuring the Volume of a Liquid

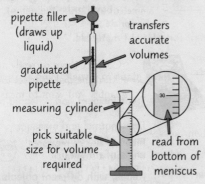

pipette filler (draws up liquid)

transfers accurate volumes

graduated pipette

measuring cylinder

pick suitable size for volume required

read from bottom of meniscus

Measuring the Volume of a Solid

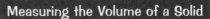

fill eureka can with water to just below spout

put the object in and collect the water in a measuring cylinder

object's volume = volume of water collected

Measuring Temperature

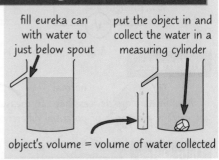

thermometer

wait for temperature to stabilise

bulb fully submerged

read off scale at eye level

Safety

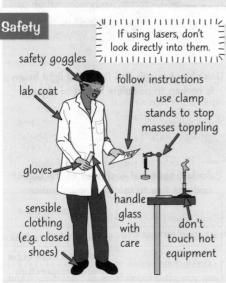

If using lasers, don't look directly into them.

safety goggles

lab coat

follow instructions

use clamp stands to stop masses toppling

gloves

sensible clothing (e.g. closed shoes)

handle glass with care

don't touch hot equipment

Measuring Mass

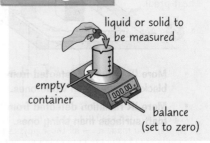

liquid or solid to be measured

empty container

balance (set to zero)

Working with Electronics

Voltmeters

Connect a voltmeter in parallel with a device to measure the potential difference across it.

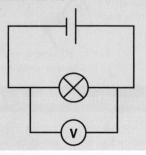

Ammeters

Connect an ammeter in series with a device to measure the current through it.

Make sure you use an ammeter or voltmeter with an appropriate scale, e.g. mA, mV.

Multimeters

Multimeters are devices that can measure current, resistance or potential difference.

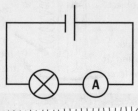

Connect them correctly and turn the dial to select the quantity you want to measure.

Light Gates

Light beam is shone from one side of light gate to detector on other side.

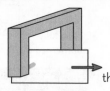

Time can also be measured with a stopwatch.

Detector sends information to computer. Computer measures time that light beam is broken by object.

Two quantities measured using light gates:

1 Speed

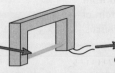

Use object length and time that light beam is broken to calculate speed of object.

object passes through light gate

2 Acceleration

Calculate speed of each part of the object and use this to calculate acceleration.

shape of object means light beam is interrupted twice

Yippee! You made it — all those physics facts and you got through them all. Bravo my friend.

PANO41